First World War
and Army of Occupation
War Diary
France, Belgium and Germany

4 CAVALRY DIVISION
Divisional Troops
Royal Army Medical Corps
Jodhpur Cavalry Field Ambulance
1 January 1917 - 28 February 1918

WO95/1158/7

The Naval & Military Press Ltd
www.nmarchive.com
Published in association with The National Archives

Published by

The Naval & Military Press Ltd

Unit 10 Ridgewood Industrial Park,

Uckfield, East Sussex,

TN22 5QE England

Tel: +44 (0) 1825 749494

www.naval-military-press.com

www.nmarchive.com

This diary has been reprinted in facsimile from the original. Any imperfections are inevitably reproduced and the quality may fall short of modern type and cartographic standards.

© **Crown Copyright**
Images reproduced by permission of The National Archives, London, England, 2015.

Contents

Document type	Place/Title	Date From	Date To
Heading	WO95/1158/7		
Heading	B E F 4 Div Troops Jodhpur Cav Fld Amb 1917 Jan To 1918 Feb To Egypt L of C Palestine		
Heading	War Diary of Jodhpur Indian Cavalry Field Ambulance 5th Cav. Div. From 1st January 1917 To 31st January 1917		
War Diary	Franleu	01/01/1917	31/01/1917
Heading	Jodhpur Cav. Field Ambulance 5th Cav. Div. Feb. 1917		
War Diary	Franleu	01/02/1917	24/02/1917
Heading	Jodhpur Cavalry Field Ambulance From 1st To 28th February 1917		
Miscellaneous	Correspondence received		
War Diary	Franleu	25/02/1917	28/02/1917
Heading	Jodhpur. Cav. F. A. Mar. 1917		
War Diary	Franleu	01/03/1917	18/03/1917
War Diary	Coulon-Villiers	19/03/1917	19/03/1917
War Diary	Halloy-Les-Pernois	20/03/1917	20/03/1917
War Diary	N.E. Albert	22/03/1917	31/03/1917
Heading	Jodhpur Cav. F. A. April 1917		
War Diary	N. E. of Albert	01/04/1917	06/04/1917
War Diary	S.E of Bihucourt	07/04/1917	09/04/1917
War Diary	Camp. S.E. of Bihucourt	10/04/1917	11/04/1917
War Diary	W. of Mory	11/04/1917	11/04/1917
War Diary	Camp S.E. of Bihucourt	12/04/1917	13/04/1917
War Diary	Camp, East of Aveluy.	14/04/1917	14/04/1917
War Diary	Bus-Les-Artois	15/04/1917	30/04/1917
Heading	Jodhpur Ind Cav Field Ambulance. May 1917		
War Diary	Bus-Les-Artois	01/05/1917	15/05/1917
War Diary	Meaulte	15/05/1917	16/05/1917
War Diary	Suzanne	16/05/1917	17/05/1917
War Diary	Le Mesnil Bruntel	18/05/1917	24/05/1917
War Diary	Camp West of Roisel	25/05/1917	31/05/1917
Heading	Jodhpur Cavalry Field Ambulance June. 1917		
War Diary	Camp West of Roisel	01/06/1917	30/06/1917
Heading	Jodhpur Cav. F. A. July 1917		
Heading	Jodhpur Cavalry Field Ambulance From 1st to 31st July 1917		
War Diary	Camp-West of Roisel	01/07/1917	01/07/1917
War Diary	L.10a.66.map 62.c.	01/07/1917	02/07/1917
War Diary	Camp West of Roisel	03/07/1917	04/07/1917
War Diary	Le-Mesnil Bruntel	05/07/1917	31/07/1917
Heading	Jodhpur Cav. F. A. Aug. 1917		
Heading	Jodhpur Cavalry Field Ambulance From 1st to 31st August 1917		
War Diary	Le-Mesnil Bruntel	01/08/1917	31/08/1917
Heading	Jodhpur Cav. F. A. Sept. 1917		
War Diary	Le-Mesnil-Bruntel	14/10/1917	30/10/1917
War Diary	Devise	31/10/1917	31/10/1917
War Diary	Le-Mesnil-Bruntel	01/10/1917	13/10/1917
War Diary	Le-Mesnil-Bruntel	01/09/1917	30/09/1917

Heading	Jodhpur Cav. F. A. Nov. 1917		
War Diary	Devise	01/11/1917	21/11/1917
War Diary	Forward Concentration Area.	21/11/1917	23/11/1917
War Diary	Devise	23/11/1917	30/11/1917
Heading	Jodhpur Cav. F. A. Dec. 1917		
War Diary	Villers-Faucon	01/12/1917	03/12/1917
War Diary	Le Mesnil Bruntel	04/12/1917	16/12/1917
War Diary	Devise	17/12/1917	31/12/1917
Heading	Jodhpur Cav. F. A. Jan. 1918		
War Diary	Camp Near Devise	01/01/1918	31/01/1918
Heading	Jodhpur Cav. F. A. February, 1918.		
War Diary	Oresmaux	08/02/1918	27/02/1918
War Diary	Camp Near Devise	01/02/1918	06/02/1918
War Diary	Guillaucourt	07/02/1918	07/02/1918
War Diary	Oresmaux	28/02/1918	28/02/1918

WO 95/11581

BEF
4 DIV TROOPS

JODHPUR CAV
FLD AMB

1917 JAN to 1918 FEB

TO EGYPT L of C PALESTINE

SERIAL No. 235.

COMMITTEE FOR THE
MEDICAL HISTORY OF THE WAR
Date 23 APR. 1917

Confidential

War Diary

of

JODHPUR INDIAN CAVALRY FIELD AMBULANCE. — 5th Cav. Div.

FROM 1st JANUARY 1917. 1916

TO 31st JANUARY 1917. 1916

Original   Medical
Army Form C. 2118.

Ref. A.D.M.S. 4th Cav.Div.
No. 63/2. of 5.1.17.

WAR DIARY of the Jodhpur Cav. Fd. Ambulance

INTELLIGENCE SUMMARY

Volume 25

(Erase heading not required.) for January 1917

Instructions regarding War Diaries and Intelligence Summaries are contained in F.S. Regs., Part II and the Staff Manual respectively. Title Pages will be prepared in manuscript.

Place	Date	Hour	Summary of Events and Information	Remarks and references to Appendices
FRANLEU	Jan 1.		Eleven men of this unit who during the past month have been doing fatigue duties at Railhead were relieved today and rejoined this unit. J.B.	
"	2nd		Nothing to record. J.B.	
"	3rd 4th 5th 6th		Nothing to record. J.B.	
"			Arranged for a room for a medical board which was held in this village today; after the medical board the D.D.M.S. of the Cavalry Corps inspected the hospital of this unit. J.B.	
"	7th 8th		Nothing to record. J.B.	
"	9th		One Lance Naik and 7 Bearers of the Army Bearer Corps – men of the Ambala Cav. Fd. Ambulance who are going to be attached to the MHOW Pioneer Battalion – were transferred to this unit temporarily under orders of the A.D.M.S. 4th Cav. Division. J.B.	

Army Form C. 2118.

WAR DIARY
INTELLIGENCE SUMMARY
(Erase heading not required.)

Place	Date	Hour	Summary of Events and Information	Remarks and references to Appendices
FRANLEU	Jan. 10		The following sum of money was paid to the Field Cashier, 4th Cav. Division for Macintoshes for this Ambulance.	
			8 Macintoshes at 23/- each for British Ranks = Francs 256 - 80 — Private property of purchasers	
			10 " " 11/6ᵈ each for Indian Ranks = 163 - 00 — " " "	
			8 " " 11/8ᵈ " " " = 130 - 40 — { Property of Jodhpur Cav. Fd Ambulance }	
			—— 550 - 20	
			26 Macintoshes	
			The sum of Francs 130 was drawn to pay for 8 macintoshes from the Indian Imperial Relief Fund. N.B.	
FRANLEU	11		One Naik and nine bearers of This Ambulance and one Lance Naik and seven bearers of The Ambala Cav. Fd Ambulance (who joined this unit yesterday) left at 4.30 am by motor lorry for Railhead, being transferred to the MHOW Pioneer Battalion. N.B.	
"	12		2ⁿᵈ Class S.A. Sweeper No. 367 K.C. VAGHELA, IS.M.D. reported his arrival for duty with this unit, being transferred from the Lucknow Cav. Fd Ambulance 4 Bearers A.B.C. who had been transferred to the Lucknow Cav. Fd Ambulance on 8ᵗʰ Dec. 1916, returned to duty with this unit. N.B.	

Army Form C. 2118.

WAR DIARY
INTELLIGENCE SUMMARY.
(Erase heading not required.)

Place	Date January	Hour	Summary of Events and Information	Remarks and references to Appendices
FRANLEU	12th		One G.S. Wagon sent to CHAUSSOY for minor repairs under orders from B.T.O. Lucknow Cav Brigade. nB	
	13th		Nothing to record. nB	
	14th		Nothing to record. nB	
	15th			
	16th		Driver H. PERKINS, ASC of this unit, reported his departure on proceeding on leave to England. nB	
	17th		Nothing to record. nB	
	18th			
	19th			
	20th		No. 631, Havildar MOTI RAWAT, 2nd/9th Gurkha Rifles, who has been Pack Store Havildar of this unit hitherto, reported his departure — being sent to O.C Reinforcements, Marseilles, to proceed to Meiran as he has been promised promotion. (Vide Memo. No. 2/2101/35 A½ 7th Jan 1916 (1917) from D.A.G, G.H.Q, 3rd Echelon, Indian Section) nB	
	21st		G.S Wagon was brought back from CHAUSSOY but no repairs had been effected except as regards the tailboard. nB	

Army Form C. 2118.

WAR DIARY
or
INTELLIGENCE SUMMARY
(Erase heading not required.)

Place	Date January	Hour	Summary of Events and Information	Remarks and references to Appendices
FRANLEU	22nd		Nothing to record. JHB	
"	23rd		G.S. Wagon sent to Divisional Repair Workshops for repairs. Private Hughes A.S.C., M.T. reported his departure on 10 days' leave.	
"	24th		Nothing to record. JHB	
"	25th			
"	26th			
"	27th		Nothing to record. JHB	
"	28th			
"	29th			
"	30th		Nothing to record JHB	
"	31st			

J.E. Bonython
Capt.
O.C. 1st/1st Wm C.F.A.

5th Cav. Div.

Following from Field Ambulance

COMMITTEE FOR THE
MEDICAL HISTORY OF THE WAR
Date 21 MAY 1917

Original Medical

Army Form C. 2118.

WAR DIARY of the Jodhpur cavalry Field Ambulance
or
INTELLIGENCE SUMMARY.
(Erase heading not required.) for the month of February 1917 — Vol. 26

Instructions regarding War Diaries and Intelligence Summaries are contained in F. S. Regs., Part II. and the Staff Manual respectively. Title pages will be prepared in manuscript.

Place	Date	Hour	Summary of Events and Information	Remarks and references to Appendices
FRANLEU	February 1917 1st 2nd 3rd 4th		Nothing to record. WB	
	5th	-	One G.S. Wagon with spare front wheel sent into ASC workshops of the Division for repairs &c. and the G.S wagon which was sent in last month with spare hind wheel returned with necessary repairs done and all the old wheels replaced. No spare wheel was sent back with the wagon. WB	
	6th 7th		Nothing to record. WB	
	8th	-	Two men of the Ambala Cav. Fd Ambulance - Acting Staff Sgt. MITCHELL and Dafadar IMMAM ALI - arrived here and are attached to this unit for a short course of instruction in Defensive Measures against Poison gases - (vide ADMS letter No. 357.) WB	
	9th	-	Nothing to record. WB	
	10th	-	Two men of the Ambala Cav. Fd. Ambulance who arrived on the 8th inst returned to their unit after the course of instruction in Defensive measures against Poison Gases. WB	

Army Form C. 2118.

WAR DIARY
or
INTELLIGENCE SUMMARY.
(Erase heading not required.)

Instructions regarding War Diaries and Intelligence Summaries are contained in F. S. Regs., Part II. and the Staff Manual respectively. Title pages will be prepared in manuscript.

Place	Date 1917	Hour	Summary of Events and Information	Remarks and references to Appendices
FRANLEU	Feb 11		Nothing to record. NB.	
	12			
	13		The following men of this unit went struck off duty & being admitted to this Ambulance as patients. Syce RAJOO SINGH, Sweeper NANOO, Lascars I.S. Lancers attached to this ambulance. NB.	
	14		Nothing to record. NB.	
	15			
	16		Nothing to record. NB.	
	17			
	18		Syce RAJOO SINGH was evacuated to the Cavalry Lucknow Cas. Clearing Station. NB	
	19		Nothing to record. NB.	
	20		Sweeper NANOO evacuated to Lucknow Cas. Clearing Stations. NB.	
	21			
	22		Nothing to record. NB.	
	23			
	24			

Medical. Serial No: **235**

Jodhpur Cavalry Field Ambulance.

From 1st to 28th February 1917.

correspondence received

General's Base Office.

oOooo---

                                Date_____

Case on which letter will be found		Initial of Ocn Su...
Main Head:	No.	

Army Form C. 2118.

WAR DIARY
or
INTELLIGENCE SUMMARY.
(Erase heading not required.)

Instructions regarding War Diaries and Intelligence Summaries are contained in F. S. Regs., Part II. and the Staff Manual respectively. Title pages will be prepared in manuscript.

Place	Date	Hour	Summary of Events and Information	Remarks and references to Appendices
FRANLEU	1917 Feb. 25th	—	One G.S. wagon, which was sent to ASC Workshops on 5th inst, was returned. MB.	
"	26th	—	In addition to collecting sick from Jodhpur Lancers, 6th Cav., Divl. Head Quarters, and RHA Brigade HtQrs — this ambulance from today collects sick from the following units — No.10 Sqdn. Machine Gun Corps, Cav. Corps Bringing Park, Field Squadron RE, and Divl. Ammunition Park. Driver H. PERKINS and Pte Lt. HUGHES returned from leave, having been detained at the Base for fatigue duties. MB	
"	27th	—	Nothing to record. MB	
"	28th	—	Nothing to record. MB	

W. Bonford Capt IMS
OC Jodhpur C.F.A.

COMMITTEE FOR THE
MEDICAL HISTORY OF THE WAR
Date -6 JUL.1917

Original
Jodhpur

Army Form C. 2118.

Vol 27

WAR DIARY of Jodhpur Cavalry Field Ambulance

INTELLIGENCE SUMMARY

(Erase heading not required.)

March 1917.

Instructions regarding War Diaries and Intelligence Summaries are contained in F. S. Regs., Part II. and the Staff Manual respectively. Title Pages will be prepared in manuscript.

Place	Date	Hour	Summary of Events and Information	Remarks and references to Appendices
FRANLEU	1st March		No. 16869 Havildar TILOK SINGH (RHA) arrived here from General Indian Base Depot to take over duties of Pack-Store Havildar vB.	
"	2nd		The D.D.M.S. of the Cavalry Corps inspected this unit. One riding horse received from O.C, A.S.C, 4th Cav Division bringing the number of riding horses up to the number authorised vB.	Q
"	3rd		Nothing to record vB.	
"	4th			
"	5th		Motor ambulance No. M 1866 went to workshops for purpose of through overhaul of engine and for the fitting of warning apparatus	
"	6th		} Nothing to record.	
"	7th			
"	8th			
"	9-10th			

Army Form C. 2118.

March 1917. WAR DIARY of Jodhpur C.27.
INTELLIGENCE SUMMARY.
(Erase heading not required.)

Instructions regarding War Diaries and Intelligence Summaries are contained in F. S. Regs., Part II. and the Staff Manual respectively. Title pages will be prepared in manuscript.

Place	Date	Hour	Summary of Events and Information	Remarks and references to Appendices
FRANLEU	March 12		Hony. Lieut. Supdt. BADRI PRASHAD was transferred to the AMBALA L.Y.A.	
Do	13		Capt. C. R. O'BRIEN I.M.S. took over charge from Capt. J. L. BOMFORD I.M.S who was ordered to proceed to ENGLAND on duty.	
Do	14		Nothing to note.	
Do	15		S.A.S. NAGINA SINGH proceeded to England on leave.	
Do	16		Nothing to note.	
Do	17		Hon. a. B.C. temporarily detached for duty with M.O.W. Prince Bullilu reported the enemy.	
Do	18		Nothing to note. Captain F.W CAMPBELL took over command of JODHPUR C.T.A. Yesterday & marched to COULON-VILLIERS	Yes
COULON-VILLIERS	19		Arrived at HALLOY-fce PERNOIS from COULON-VILLIERS	
Do				

Army Form C. 2118.

WAR DIARY of Jodhpur Cavalry Field Ambulance

March 1917

INTELLIGENCE SUMMARY

(Erase heading not required.)

Place	Date	Hour	Summary of Events and Information	Remarks and references to Appendices
HALLOY-Es-PERNOIS	21st		Marched from HALLOY to point 1500 yards N.E. of ALBERT	A/G
N.E. ALBERT	22nd		No 2430 Bearer GIWAN 2nd A.B.C. admitted for Mumps & T.A. Evacuated Sick.	A/G
"	23rd			
"	24th			
"	25th		nil to report	A/G
"	26th			
"	27th			
"	28th			
"	29th			
"	30th			
"	31st		Asst Surgeon Nagina Singh reported for duty from leave in Gt Britain 6 Aug. Owned private Kraft: Above troops now Rawalpindi Bde known from Jodhpur Lancers to day.	A/G

Jus Campbell Capt RAMC
O.C. Jodhpur C.F.A.

COMMITTEE FOR THE
MEDICAL HISTORY OF THE WAR

Date −6 JUL. 1917

Army Form C. 2118.

WAR DIARY of Original Jodhpur Cav. Bd.
INTELLIGENCE SUMMARY Field Ambulance, Vol 28

for April 1917

(Erase heading not required.)

Place	Date	Hour	Summary of Events and Information	Remarks and references to Appendices
N.E. of ALBERT	1st 1917		One Sweeper – MF/2030 JHANDOO – S&T Corps arrived as a reinforcement to this unit, from the base. Capt T.L.BOMFORD IMS – returned from duty in England in the evening. w.B	
"	2nd		Capt. F.W. CAMPBELL R.A.M.C. being relieved by Capt T.L.BOMFORD returned to duty with the Lucknow C.F.A. w.B.	
"	3rd		Nothing to record w.B	
"	4th			
"	5th			
S.E. of BIHUCOURT	6th		The Ambulance marched at 10 a.m. via the ALBERT – BAPAUME road and arrived at camp South East of BIHUCOURT at 3.30 p.m. w.B.	
	7th		Nothing to record. w.B	
	8th		ABC Bearer No.7631 RAM SAHAI admitted to this unit accidentally by the an explosion occurring while he was working his foot – at 7.15 p.m. w.B.	
	9th		Orders received in the evening for marching to a position of readiness early next morning. w.B.	

Army Form C. 2118.

WAR DIARY
Jodhpur Cav. Fd. Ambulance.

INTELLIGENCE SUMMARY

April 1917. p.2

Place	Date	Hour	Summary of Events and Information	Remarks
Camp S.E. of BIHUCOURT	April 10	5am	Marched from camp, leaving behind B. echelon, towards a position of readiness, at the waiting place for the Division, on the BAPAUME–SAPIGNIES road halted, with other units of the Division. Division received orders to return to camp.	
"	"	8am	Arrived in camp. Bearer THAKURI - ? No. 7 A.B.C.Coy attached to this unit was evacuated sick to Lucknow C.C.S.	
"	"	5pm	Orders received that Division must be ready to move at one hour's notice – mB.	
"	11th	7am	Marched via SAPIGNIES, ERVILLERS to country ground west of MORY (Map 57c B 20 b) where the Lucknow and Ambala Cav. Fd. Ambulances also camped with A2 Echelon of the Division	
W. of MORY	"	5pm	Orders received from the Officer in charge of A Echelon to return to camp at BIHUCOURT. Marched and arrived in camp at 9pm. mB	
Camp S.E. of BIHUCOURT	12th	10am	Orders received that Division is placed on two hours' notice to be ready to move. mB	
"	13th		Ambulance marched at 10.45 am via IRLES, MIRAUMONT, to camp East of AVELUY. The Water Cart (a civilian wagon with tank) was left behind in camp – having broken down on the previous day. mB.	

WAR DIARY · Jodhpur Cav. Fd. Ambulance

April 1917 · P3 · Army Form C. 2118.

INTELLIGENCE SUMMARY
(Erase heading not required.)

Place	Date	Hour	Summary of Events and Information	Remarks and references to Appendices
Camp East RAVELUY.	14th	—	Ambulance marched at 11 a.m. with B Echelon of Lucknow Cav Brigade via BOUZINCOURT to camp at BUS-LES-ARTOIS. ref.	
BUS-LES-ARTOIS	15th	—	Nothing to record. ref.	
"	16th			
"	17th		Nothing to record ref	
"	18th			
"	19th	—	Twenty two men of this ambulance were inoculated with antityphoid serum T.A.B. one oc. dose. ref.	
"	20th		Nothing to record ref.	
"	21st		Bearer CHITER SINGH was evacuated sick from this unit to No. 3 Canadian Stationary Hospital – with fever of uncertain origin – possibly due to Tubercularis? ref.	
"	22nd	—	Nothing to record ref	
"	23rd			
"	24th	—	Nothing to record ref.	
"	25th			
"	26th	—	S.A.S. Vaghela of this unit was admitted as a patient to the Hospital of this unit – suffering from piles. ref.	

WAR DIARY

Jodhpur Cav. Fd. Ambulance

INTELLIGENCE SUMMARY

April 1917 P.4

Place	Date April	Hour	Summary of Events and Information	Remarks and references to Appendices
BUS-LES-ARTOIS	26th		Water cart received from Ordnance to replace the water cart which broke down and was left at BIHUCOURT.	
"	27th		Motor ambulance M↑1868 partially broke the bracket which fixes the rear hind spring to the frame. Nothing to record. n.B.	
"	28th		Motor ambulance M↑1866 broke the drop-arm of the steering levers - The drop arm was replaced by a new one during the evening. n.B.	
"	29th		L. Dafadar JAWAHIR SINGH of the Jodhpur I.S. Lancers who has been attached to this unit as Transport driver has returned to duties with the Regiment and Sowar No. 1674 QAYAR KHAN of the Jodhpur I.S. Lancers has been taken on the strength from this date as transport driver. Sweeper SAGWA - S.&T.Corps No. Mt/678 arrived as a reinforcement for this unit - bringing the establishment of Sweepers for this unit up to 3 which is one more than authorised. n.B.	
"	30th		Nothing to record n.B.	

V. Branford Capt I.M.S.
O.C. Jodhpur Cav. Fd. Ambulance

Jodhpur Bar Field Ambulance

COMMITTEE FOR THE
MEDICAL HISTORY OF THE WAR
Date 27 JUL 1917

medical

Original

WAR DIARY of Jodhpur Cavalry Fd. Ambulance (Army Form C.2118)

INTELLIGENCE SUMMARY

(Erase heading not required.)

For May - 1917

Vol. 29

Instructions regarding War Diaries and Intelligence Summaries are contained in F.S. Regs., Part II. and the Staff Manual respectively. Title pages will be prepared in manuscript.

Place	Date May	Hour	Summary of Events and Information	Remarks and references to Appendices
BUS-LES -ARTOIS	1st		⎱ Nothing to record. ps.	
"	2nd		⎰	
"	3rd		S.A.S. VAGHELA was transferred as a patient to No.3 Canadian Stationary Hospital. ps.	
"	4th		Nothing to record. ps.	
"	5th		Nothing to record. ps.	
"	6th		Two Bearers of the Army Bearer Corps joined this unit as reinforcements. Company / No. / Name. 5th / 5157 / HALKA 7th / 17497 / HARKISHAN. ps.	
"	7th		Nothing to record. ps.	
"	8th		ABC. Bearer HALKA - was transferred to Lucknow C.F.A. with which unit he had previously served - and the following Bearer was transferred from the Lucknow CFA to join this unit. 7th Coy A.B.C. Bearer No. 17007 CHADAMMI. ps.	
"	9th		⎱	
"	10th		⎰ Nothing to record. ps.	
	11th			

Army Form C. 2118

WAR DIARY for May 1917 — (P.2.)

INTELLIGENCE SUMMARY of Jodhpur Cav. Fd. Ambulance

(Erase heading not required.)

Instructions regarding War Diaries and Intelligence Summaries are contained in F. S. Regs., Part II. and the Staff Manual respectively. Title pages will be prepared in manuscript.

Place	Date May	Hour	Summary of Events and Information	Remarks and references to Appendices
BUS-LES-ARTOIS	12th	—	Nothing to record. n.B.	
" "	13th	—	Fifteen men (in charge of the Pack Store Havildar) were sent to the Camp of the Dismounted men of the Division and will be moved to the new area by train — (Vide 4th Cav. Div. A.A. & Q.M.G's Orders Q.7120 and Q.7123 and A.D.M.S' No. 1965) n.B.	Lucknow Cav. Brigade Operation Order No. 1. of 14. May 1917
" "	14th	—	Nothing to record. n.B.	
" "	15th	—	Marched at 6:15 am., via ACHEUX, ALBERT to camp at eastern end of MEAULTE, arriving at 11 am. n.B.	
MEAULTE.	16th	—	Marched at 7 am. via FRICOURT, MARICOURT to camp north of SUZANNE arriving at 11 am. n.B.	
SUZANNE	17th	—	Marched at 9.15 am - via MARICOURT, CLERY (Halting for one hour to water and feed), PERONNE to camp west of LE MESNIL BRUNTEL, arriving at 4.30 p.m. n.B.	
LE MESNIL BRUNTEL	18th 19th 20th	—	Nothing to record. n.B.	
"	21st	—	One Sweeper SAGWA S. & T. Corps, who was Supernumerary in this ambulance, was transferred to Lucknow Cav. Fd. Ambulance. n.B. Nothing to record. n.B.	
"	22nd	—	Nothing to record. n.B.	

Army Form C. 2118

WAR DIARY for May 1917 (P.3)
INTELLIGENCE SUMMARY of Jodhpur Cav. Fd. Ambulance

(Erase heading not required.)

Place	Date May	Hour	Summary of Events and Information	Remarks and references to Appendices
LE MESNIL BRUNTEL	23rd	—	The ambulance is 'closed' from to-day. WB.	
"	24th	—	The ambulance marched at 9 am — following the transport echelons of the Lucknow Cav. Brigade, via CARTIGNY and HANCOURT to camp west of ROISEL (Map 62c — at K.21.b.3.9.) The four CSL tents provided for this unit were brought along to the new camp and one G.S. wagon was sent back in the evening to bring along stores left behind. WB.	
Camp West of ROISEL	25th	—	Nothing to record. WB.	
"	26th	—		
"	27th	—	Collection of sick by this unit is extended to collecting sick from all units of the Lucknow Cav. Bde. in this area. WB.	
"	28th	—	Nothing to record. WB.	
"	29th	—	The camp was of this unit was moved one hundred yards south - to be further from the railway which was shelled to-day. WB.	
"	30th	—	Sowar GAYAR KHAN of the Jodhpur I.S. Lancers — attached to this unit was evacuated to the Secunderabad Cav. Fd. Ambulance - having a sprained ankle. WB.	
"	31st	—	Nothing to record. WB.	

WBoughton Capt IMS
OC Jodhpur CFA.
M

June 1917

Joffre's Leading Field Ambulance

medical

ORIGINAL

WAR DIARY of Jodhpur C.F.A.

Army Form C. 2118.

Volume 30

For June 1917.

INTELLIGENCE SUMMARY.

(Erase heading not required.)

Place	Date June	Hour	Summary of Events and Information	Remarks and references to Appendices
Camp West of ROISEL	1st		The Ambulance paraded for inspection by D.D.M.S. Cavalry Corps. nB	
"	2nd		Nothing to record. nB	
"	3rd		The D.D.M.S. Cavalry Corps visited this unit. nB	
"	4th		The undermentioned follower, attached to this unit in place of a Cook of the Supply and Transport Corps, was evacuated sick to sickness this unit. Name Regtl No. PURBHU (Follower) 19 Jodhpur I.S. Lancers Cook.	nB
"	5th 6th 7th 8th		Nothing to record. nB	
"	9th 10th 11th 12th 13th		One L.D. Mule died this morning of colic. nB Nothing to record. nB	
"	14th		No. T/35509 Driver A.R. MARR joined this unit as a Transport Driver (vide C.260 dated 13-6-17 from Adjutant, A.S.C. 4th Cav. Div.) nB.	
"	15th		Nothing to record. nB	
"	16th		Nothing to record. nB	

Army Form C. 2118.

June - 1917. Jodhpur p(2)

WAR DIARY

INTELLIGENCE SUMMARY. Jodhpur Cav. Fd. Ambulance

(Erase heading not required.)

Instructions regarding War Diaries and Intelligence Summaries are contained in F. S. Regs., Part II. and the Staff Manual respectively. Title pages will be prepared in manuscript.

Place	Date	Hour	Summary of Events and Information	Remarks and references to Appendices
Camp West of ROISEL	June 17th		Nothing to record. nB	
"	18th		}	
"	19th		}	
"	20th		} Nothing to record. nB	
"	21st		}	
"	22nd		}	
"	23rd		}	
"	24th		}	
"	25th		8 men of the Army Bearer Corps - detailed for fatigue duty to road repair to stay nB	
"	26th		Motor ambulance No. M.T. 1868 broke two cogs of its crown wheel. nB	
			The same fatigue party was detailed to duty to stay as yesterday. Motor ambulance No. M.T. 1868 went to workshop for repair in charge of 1 Corpl GOODMAN nB	
"	27th		A party of 4 men of the Army Bearer Corps completed the work which they had been doing the two previous days.	
			The following reinforcements arrived :- No. 7. A.B.Coy. No. 7612 Bearer THAKURI } Both of whom have served previously in this unit. nB. No. 2. A.B.Coy. No. 2430 " JEWAN	
"	28th		Nothing to record nB	
"	29th		Nothing to record nB	
"	30th		Sowar GAYAR KHAN of the Jodhpur & S. Lancers - attached to this unit - returned from the Lucknow E.C.S. being now fit for duty.	

M Romfret Capt I.M.S.
O.C. Jodhpur C.F.A.

COMMITTEE FOR THE
MEDICAL HISTORY OF THE WAR
Date   16 OCT. 1917

"Medical."   Serial No. 235.

Jodhpur Cavalry Field Ambulance.

From 1st to 31st July 1917.

Medical
Army Form C. 2118.
Original
WAR DIARY of Jodhpur C.F.A.
INTELLIGENCE SUMMARY.
for July 1917.
Volume 31

Place	Date	Hour	Summary of Events and Information	Remarks and references to Appendices
Camp West of ROISEL	July 1st	6.30 a.m.	The "Emergency Bearer Party" (as laid down in A.D.M.S. 4th Cav. Div. No. 2504 of 11.6.1917) assembled at K.21.b.3.9. (Map 62.c) with the exception of 10 Bearers of the Army Bearer Corps of the Lucknow Cav. Fd. Ambulance who joined the party later on at TEMPLEUX LE GUÉRARD. This party and the medical equipment were taken to TEMPLEUX LE GUÉRARD by motor and horsed ambulances and by G.S. and limbered wagon.	
L.10.a.6.6. Map 62.c		9.0 a.m.	The O.C. Emergency Bearer Party reported his arrival to the O.C. B.M subsector of the line held by the 4th Cav. Division and handed over to Capt. HILL, R.A.M.C., M.O. of Inniskilling Dragoons, and to S.A.S. MOHAMMED AHMED, attached to 38th Central India Horse, the men and equipment detailed in ADMS 4th Cav. Div. No. 2992 of 29.6.1917. During the remainder of the day men and equipment were brought up from TEMPLEUX to the Regimental aid post at B.M subsector Headquarters, in small parties; 2 gallons of water were sterilised and a few instruments and dressings, morphia, optinub, etc. were made ready; and arrangements made for providing hot drinks and comforts.	
"		8 p/m	Motor hoards were put up directing walking wounded to the Divisional collecting station at TEMPLEUX.	
"		9.30 p/m	Two horsed ambulances left the camp of Jodhpur C.F.A. and reported to O.C. Emergency Bearer Party at 10.30 p/m. They were kept in readiness in partial shelter 300 yards from the Regimental Aid Post. These ambulances brought up a supply of blankets. JWB	

Army Form C. 2118.

WAR DIARY
INTELLIGENCE SUMMARY.
(Erase heading not required.)

for July

Place	Date	Hour	Summary of Events and Information	Remarks and references to Appendices
L.10.a.b.6 Map 12.c.	July 2	12.56 am	Bombardment of Cologne Farm started.	
"		1.50 am	One German prisoner brought in to have a wound dressed.	
"		2.15 am	The first wounded of the attacking party arrived. Of the attacking party 32 men of the Inniskilling Dragoons and 1 Sapper R.E. were attended to by the Emergency Bearer Party; of these 20 had already received attention at the advanced regimental aid posts from Capt Hill Rame and from F.A.S. Mohammed Ahmad. Capt Hardy Rame, M.D. 17th Lancers also assisted in attending to the wounded at B III Ambulance Headquarters. The severely wounded were taken to the Divisional Collecting Station in the wheeled stretcher carriages; the horsed ambulance wagons made 3 journeys to the Divisional Collecting Station with some severely wounded. The horsed ambulance wagons were sent back to the goodpour C.Y.A. Camp at about 5.30 am at which time it was somewhat misty.	
"		6.45 am	A provisional estimate — of Chevalliers who went to the v.c. ambulls ear F.A. ambulance who was at Divisional Collecting Station, for transmission to the A.D.M.S. The last wounded to arrive was about 7 pm	
"		11.0 am	The work of the Emergency Bearer Party being complete, the O.C. B III Ambulance gave instructions that the party should leave in the evening.	

Army Form C. 2118.

WAR DIARY
or
INTELLIGENCE SUMMARY.

(Erase heading not required.)

2nd July —

Instructions regarding War Diaries and Intelligence Summaries are contained in F. S. Regs., Part II. and the Staff Manual respectively. Title pages will be prepared in manuscript.

Place	Date	Hour	Summary of Events and Information	Remarks and references to Appendices
	July 2		A message was sent to Jeudhine C.F.A. to provide transport for removing men and equipment of the party from TEMPLEUX and messages were sent to O.C.'s walkers and bearers and another C.F.A. stating that their men and equipment would be at K.21 b.3.9. Trip 62 c at 11 p.m. The rest of the day was spent in making preparations for the return of the party and in helping to dress the wounds of, and to evacuate, a few men who received wounds during the afternoon.	
		6.30 p.m.	A small party of the men & equipment of the Emergency Bearer Party left the Regimental Aid Post.	
		11 p.m.	The Emergency B. Party was back at K.21 b.3.9. And their men & equipment were fetched by the cars of the Field and bearers C.F.A.'s. N.B.	
Cande Hecl of RUISEL	3	—	Motor Ambulance MA1866 practically broke the near hind spring. The spring of the	
	4	—	Motor Ambulance was replaced by a new one obtained by the workshops N.B.	
LE-MESNIL BRUNTEL	5		The Ambulance marched at 9.30 a.m. across country to the camps at LE-MESNEL-BRUNTEL — arriving at 12 noon — Motor Ambulance MA1868 turned from workshops with a new crown wheel. From 12 noon this ambulance was used for the reception of sick (i.e. the admission and discharge of sick as reported but cases are transferred as there is no accommodation for them in the camp) N.B.	

Army Form C. 2118.

WAR DIARY for July '17
or
INTELLIGENCE SUMMARY.
(Erase heading not required.)

Instructions regarding War Diaries and Intelligence Summaries are contained in F.S. Regs., Part II. and the Staff Manual respectively. Title pages will be prepared in manuscript.

Place	Date July	Hour	Summary of Events and Information	Remarks and references to Appendices
LE-MESNIL BRUNTEL	7th		Nothing to record. n.B.	
"	8th		Nothing to record. n.B.	
"	9th		Bearer No. 8815 (3rd Coy) WANG CHOOK A.B.C. returned to this unit as reinforcement n.B.	
"	10th		Nothing to record. n.B.	
"	11th		One L.D. Mule evacuated to Lucknow Base M.V.S. suffering from cardiac debility n.B.	
"	12th 13th		} Nothing to record n.B.	
"	14th		One L.D. Horsed Ambulance wagon sent to A.S.C. workshops for repairs n.B.	
"	15th		One riding horse and one L.D. horse received to replace wastage — The L.D. Horse is quite unsuitable for the work of this ambulance n.B.	
"	16th		# No. T/33520 Driver A.N. WELSH, A.S. Corps reported his arrival from the A.S.C. 4th Cav. Div. n.B.	
"	17th 18th 19th		Driver S.H. BURBECK A.S.C. (acting L/Corporal) left this unit being transferred to the 18th Reserve Park, TR. L". Horsed Ambulance returned from workshops being repaired. 2.2 L". Horsed Ambulance sent to A.S.C. workshops for repairs. n.B	

Army Form C. 2118.

WAR DIARY for July 1917.
INTELLIGENCE SUMMARY.
(Erase heading not required.)

Instructions regarding War Diaries and Intelligence Summaries are contained in F.S. Regs., Part II. and the Staff Manual respectively. Title pages will be prepared in manuscript.

Place	Date July	Hour	Summary of Events and Information	Remarks and references to Appendices
LE MESNIL BRUNTEL	20	—	Nothing to record. nB	
"	21st	—	No. 14/16/63s - Sergeant Perrott a/a H.T. evacuated to Ambulen C.F.A. suffering from Bronchitis nB	
"	22nd	—	Nothing to record. nB	
"	23rd	—	Ward orderly, Pion Sergt 37/h Dancers, Water carrier, Shavers s+T corps, Sweepers, Shavers s+T corps. detailed for duty with the medical officers of the working party of 4th C. Division nB	
"	24th 25th	—	} Nothing to record. nB	
"	26th 27th 28th	—	} Nothing to record. nB	
"	29th	—	No. d.3/027525 - Sergeant HURDLEY, W.E of a/a H.T. reported his arrival for duty with two men from Ambulen C.F.A. nB.	
"	30th 31st	—	Nothing to record. nB	

V. Bowfield
Chaplain 1st class
O/C Jodhpur C.F.A.

COMMITTEE FOR THE
MEDICAL HISTORY OF THE WAR
Date 16 OCT. 1917

"Medical".   Serial No: **235.**

Jodhpur Cavalry Field Ambulance.

From 1st to 31st August 1917.

Medical
Army Form C. 2118.
Vol 32

ORIGINAL

WAR DIARY of Jodhpur C.F.A.

for August 1917

or

INTELLIGENCE SUMMARY.

(Erase heading not required.)

Instructions regarding War Diaries and Intelligence Summaries are contained in F. S. Regs., Part II. and the Staff Manual respectively. Title pages will be prepared in manuscript.

Place	Date August	Hour	Summary of Events and Information	Remarks and references to Appendices
LE-MESNIL BRUNTEL	1st	—	Captain T. L. Bomford proceeded on 10 days leave to U.K. Light Horse ambulance returned from workshops being repaired. RMc	
"	2nd	—	Nothing to record. RMc	
"	3rd	—	Took over charge of Jodhpur C.F.A. Ambulance Capt Rame RMc	
"	4th	—	No.04/16/8 35 Serjeant Rivett R&C. H.T. rejoined the unit after being discharged from Hospital. One L.D. Horse being quite unsuitable for this unit exchanged from 4th Cav. A.H. transferred unit for L.D. Mule. One L.D. Mule received to replace wastage. RMc	
"	5th	—	Capt Rawling RMc at Ambulance Cdr rejoined this unit.	
"	6th	—	No.47 dfsr BIRJU (private-servant of Captain Bomford Sms) killed by lightning. RMc	
"	7th	—	No.04/16/13 Serjt Rivett RSA H.T. being surplus to strength, transferred to Lucknow C.F.A. under orders of O.C. A.D.S. 4 F.C. Div. RMc	
"	8th,9th,10th	—	Nothing to record. RMc	
"	11th,12th	—	Nothing to record. RMc	
"	13th,14th	—	Nothing to record. RMc	

Army Form C. 2118.

For August 1917 WAR DIARY

INTELLIGENCE SUMMARY.

(Erase heading not required.)

Instructions regarding War Diaries and Intelligence Summaries are contained in F.S. Regs., Part II. and the Staff Manual respectively. Title pages will be prepared in manuscript.

Place	Date August	Hour	Summary of Events and Information	Remarks and references to Appendices
LE-MESNIL BRUNTEL	15-16-17	—	Nothing to record. RMM	
,,	18-19	—	One driver A.S.C. H.T. inoculated against Enterica fever. 1st C.C. first dose. RMM N.O. Ramtanuj Bhist Khairati regained unit from divisional working party. RMM Sweeper Ghasitoo	
,,	20, 21st	—	Nothing to record. A/B	
,,	22nd	—	No 33157 Bearer MAHABIR, A.B.C. No 44647 Cook RAM SAROOP, A+T Corps Joined as reinforcement from Marcelles. A/B	
,,	23rd, 24	—	Nothing to record. RMM	
,,	25, 26, 27, 28	—	Nothing to record. RMM	
,,	29	—	Driver A.S.C. had 2nd dose of T.A.B. Vaccine (I.C.C.) A/B	
,,	30, 31st	—	Nothing to record. Except Capt Bomford Jones did not return from leave to U.K. A/B	

Asst J. Bonner
Capt Rao C
acting D.E. Jodhpur C.L.A

COMMITTEE FOR THE
MEDICAL HISTORY OF THE WAR
Date 12 DEC. 1917

Army Form C. 2118.

WAR DIARY of Jodhpur e.F.A.

INTELLIGENCE SUMMARY.

for October 1917

(Erase heading not required.)

Place	Date October 1917	Hour	Summary of Events and Information	Remarks and references to Appendices
LE-MESNIL-BRUNTEL	14th	—	S.A.S. Nagmt Sinjf returned from leave to Paris. n/B	
	15th, 16th	—	Nothing to record. n/B	
	17th	—	No 7609 Bearer Shera A.B.C., evacuated sick. n/B	
	18th, 19th, 20th	—	Nothing to record. n/B	
	21st, 22nd, 23rd, 24th	—	Nothing to record. n/B	
	25th	—	4 men of the A.B.C. proceeded to ATHIES for duty, instead of 3 men and will continue in future. n/B	
	26th, 27th	—	Nothing to record. n/B	
	28th, 29th, 30th	—	Nothing to record. n/B	
DEVISE.	31st	—	The Ambulance moved to the site of its erection. The new camp which is in process of erection. The horse standings have been completed — but no huts for the men have as yet arrived to be put up. Consequently the men are accommodated either in tents or improvised shelters.	

M Bomford Capt I.M.S.
O.C. Jodhpur C.F.A.

Medical

Original

Army Form C. 2118.

235 Volume 34

For October 1917 WAR DIARY of Jodhpur O.I.A.

INTELLIGENCE SUMMARY.

(Erase heading not required.)

Place	Date 1917	Hour	Summary of Events and Information	Remarks and references to Appendices
LE-MESNIL-BRUNTEL	1st		8 men of The Army Bearer Corps sent to ATHIES for fatigue duties at The Camp which is being prepared. 10 men of This antedrome under a N.C.O. sent to prepare a camp site for this mission	
	2nd		Working parties continued work - as yesterday - and will so continue.	n.B.
	3rd 4th 5th 6th 7th 8th		Nothing to record n.B.	
	9th		Nothing to record n.B.	
	9th 10th		No. 999 1st Class S/A.S. NAGINA SINGH proceeded to PARIS on leave. Instead of 8 men, in future only 3 men, of the ABC proceed to ATHIES for duty. n.B.	n.B.
	11th 12th		Nothing to record n.B.	
	13th		Two remounts arrived - (one pony and one L.D. horse) n.B.	

Original

Medical

WAR DIARY of Jodhpur C.F.A.

INTELLIGENCE SUMMARY

For September 1917

Army Form C. 2118.

Serial No. 23 Vol 33

Place	Date	Hour	Summary of Events and Information	Remarks and references to Appendices
LE-MESNIL-BRUNTEL	1st 2nd 3rd	—	Nothing to record.	
"	4th	—	Took over charge of Jodhpur C.F.A. WBonsfor	
"	5th to 12th	—	Nothing to record.	
"	13th	—	One I.D. Horse evacuated sick (oedema of hind limbs) WBA	Authority R.O. No 42.1115 24/4-7-17 140000 4 C. Div and Corr copies No AMD/S09/16 of 12.9.17
"	14th	—	~~Nothing to record.~~ S.A.S. NAGINA SINGH, I.S.M.D. Awarded Meritorious Service Medal. WBA	
"	15th to 18th	—	Nothing to record. WBA	
"	19th	—		
"	20th	—	One riding horse, cast by the D.D.R., evacuated. WBA	
"	21st	—	One G.S. wagon, 2 drivers H.S. & fives I.D Mules attached for temporary duty with Pioneer Batt 1st Cav Div. WBA	
"	22nd	—	Nothing to record.	
"	23rd	=	Captain T.L. Bomford rejoined & resumed charge of the unit. WB His leave in England having been extended owing to sickness.	
"	24th 25th 26th	—	Nothing to record. WB	
"	27th 28th	—	Nothing to record. WB	
"	29th 30th	—	Nothing to record. WB	

W Bomford
Capt. IMS
OC Jodhpur Cav Fd Ambulance

COMMITTEE FOR THE
MEDICAL HISTORY OF THE WAR
Date 8 FEB. 1918

Goodfellow. Capt. F. A.

Nov. 1917

Original

Medical

WAR DIARY of Jodhpur C.F.A.

INTELLIGENCE SUMMARY

for November 1917

Army Form C. 2118.
Volume 35
233

Place	Date 11/1917	Hour	Summary of Events and Information	Remarks and references to Appendices
DEVISE	1st	—	Nothing to record. WB	
	2nd	—	No G.S. wagon Twitham evacuated sick. WB	
	3rd	—	One G.S. wagon sent to A.S.C workshops for repairs. One motor ambulance went to workshops to be fitted with warning apparatus for interior. WB	
	4th	—	Nothing to record. WB	
	5th	—		
	6th	—		
	7th	—	Nothing to record. WB	
	8th	—		
	9th	—	Meerut No 11672. Sweeper LABHOO S+J Corps, joined the unit as reinforcement. WB.	
	10th	—	Nothing to record. WB	
	11th	—	The G.S. wagon Twitham with necessary repairs effected. WB	
	12th	—	The motor ambulance returned from workshop fitted with warning apparatus. WB	
	13th	—	No 1094 Farrier Peetlaraching Jodhpur S.S. Lancers, attacked Jodhpur O.F.A. consentrioial. WB	
	14th	—	Nothing to record. WB	
	15th	—	H.S. keeper Ganri Shanker S+J Corps were sent on leave to Paris (? days). WB Head orderly Canna Pul B.S.J. Horses	
	16th	—	Nothing to record. WB	
	17th	—	Nov. Driver Welsh, A.S.C. 9 this unit was evacuated sick. WB	
	18th	—	The Lugha G.S. Wagon was returned for duty of this unit. The spokes of the near side wheels were loose and need repair. WB	

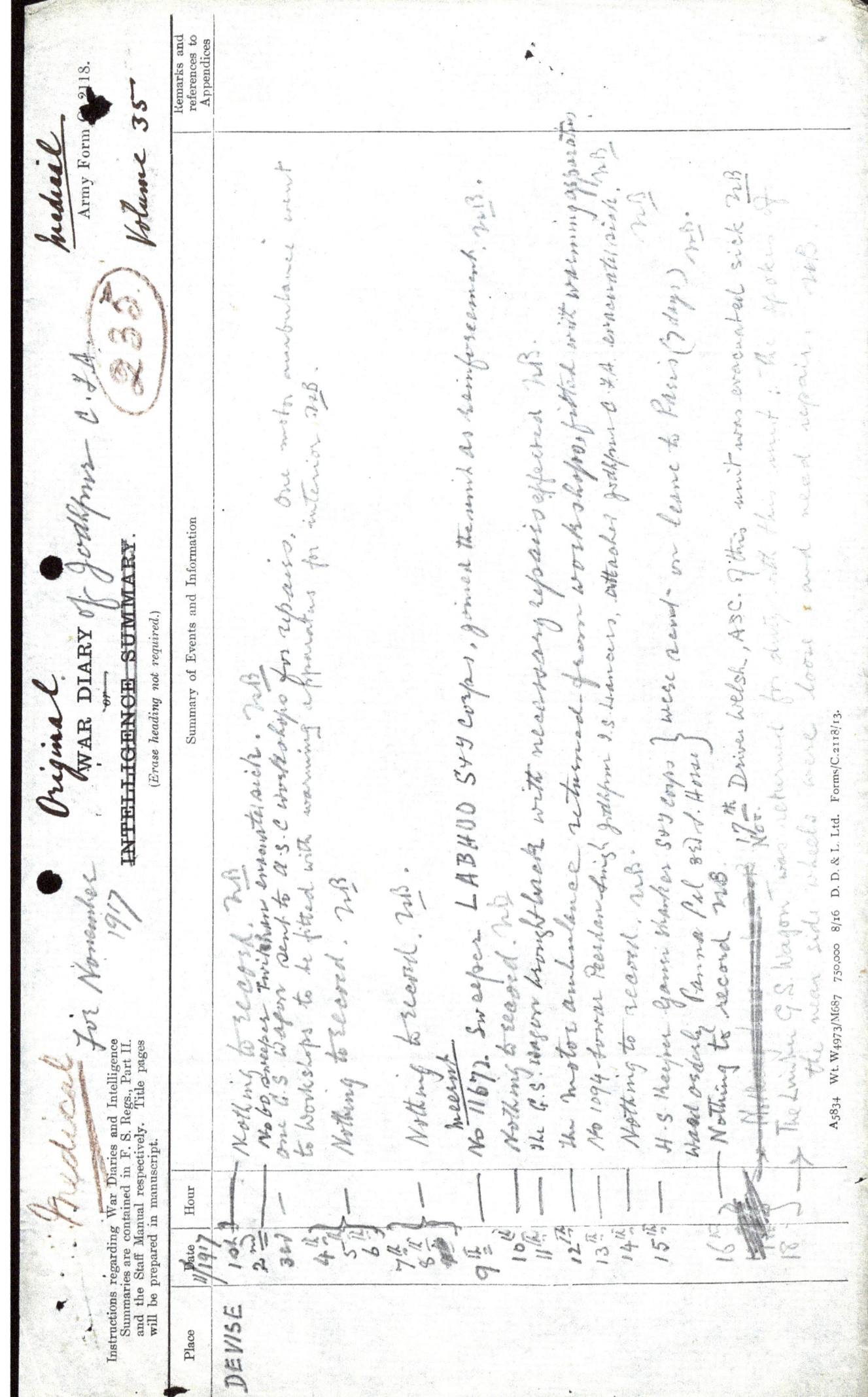

Army Form C.2118.

WAR DIARY
or
INTELLIGENCE SUMMARY.
(Erase heading not required.)

Place	Date Nov	Hour	Summary of Events and Information	Remarks and references to Appendices
DEVISE	19	—	In accordance with Operation Order No.1 of 17/11/1917 from the A.D.M.S. 4th Cav. Div. – this ambulance was placed under the orders of O.C. Ambala Cav. Fd. Ambulance pro. tem. in the case of a major – in RG departure of the Lucknow Cav. Brigade. Orders were received to be ready to march from 3.30 am tomorrow. m.B.	
"	20th	—	Standing ready for marching. m.B.	
"	21st	3.15 am	Received orders to march to concentration area of The Division.	
Moved to Concentration area	"	12.30 pm	Arrived in concentration area – 8 7 men of the A.B.C. marched on foot.	
"	"	3 pm	Motor ambulance N9 1868 Sent to Workshops on account of a spring broken on the march today.	
"	22nd	—	No 91196 Bearer Murad A.B.C. 9th Coy, annual Trick and motor ambulance No 1868 returned from workshops fitted with new spring. m.B.	
"	23rd	—	Marched from camp at 12 noon and returned to Camp at DEVISE arriving at 5 pm. One mule lame. m.B.	
DEVISE.	24th	—	No 91196/2030 Sweeper Khandos I.V.S. expd. unmatricck. m.B.	

Army Form C.2118.

WAR DIARY
or
INTELLIGENCE SUMMARY.
(Erase heading not required.)

Instructions regarding War Diaries and Intelligence Summaries are contained in F.S. Regs., Part II. and the Staff Manual respectively. Title pages will be prepared in manuscript.

Place	Date Nov 1917	Hour	Summary of Events and Information	Remarks and references to Appendices
DEVISE	25th	3.45 am	Received orders to march from camp.	
		5.45 am	Marched from camp and proceeded to a concentration area at VILLERS-FAUCON - arriving at 12.45 p.m.	
		3 pm	Marched from VILLERS-FAUCON to camp at DEVISE arriving at 7 p.m. The dismounted men of the unit on the return march were carried by lorry. MB.	
"	26th		A.B.Corps Bearer BHAGAT RAM (No. ¾ I.E.Coy) evacuated sick. MB	
"	27th		Driver C. Penrose A.S.C., H.T. (No. T4/185137) arrived as a reinforcement being transferred from Sialkot Cav. Fd. Ambulance. MB.	
"	28th		Driver C. PENROSE sent to Ambulance for treatment - MB.	
"	29th		Nothing to record. MB.	
"	30th		Received orders at 11.30 a.m. to move with the Division - and arrived at camp at VILLERS-FAUCON at 6 pm.	

M Bonford Capt. IMS
OC - Jodhpur Cav. Fd. Ambulance

Jodhpur cav., J. a.

Dec. 1917.

Medical

ORIGINAL

WAR DIARY of Jodhpur S.G. for December 1917

INTELLIGENCE SUMMARY

Army Form C. 2118

(Volume 36) 235

Place	Date 1917 December	Hour	Summary of Events and Information	Remarks and references to Appendices
VILLERS-FAUCON	1st	5 am	Captain T.L. Bomford I.M.S. was detached from this ambulance for duty with Divisional Headquarters. This ambulance was attached for administrative purposes to the Sialkot C.F. Ambulance.	
		12 noon	A Bearer Division of this ambulance consisting of 12 Bearers ₹ IV, A.B. Corps and the Lighthorsed ambulance wagons accompanied ₹ IV Bearer Division of the Sialkot C.Y.A. in order to help in the evacuation of wounded - but being found not to be necessary they ordered back to the camp where they arrived at about 4 pm. T.B.	
"	2nd		Between midnight and 2 am, one pony of this unit strayed from the lines of the Divisional Headquarters. Nothing else to record. T.B.	
"	3rd		The ambulance marched at 7.30 am, when Capt. T.L. Bomford I.M.S. and the ward orderly rejoined the unit, and arrived in camp at LE MESNIL BRUNTEL at 3 pm. The starting handle and lever of one of the ambulance cars was broken. T.B.	
LE MESNIL BRUNTEL	4th		A new starting handle and lever was fixed on the ambulance car at the workshops of the Div. Supply Column. T.B. Driver C. PENROSE, A.S.C., M.T. returned to this unit. T.B.	
"	5th		No. MT/2037 Sweeper KHACHERU S, M.T. Corps transferred to Thi. unit to duty from the Sanitary Section 4th Cav. Divn. and No. 4269 B² BHAGAT RAM, A.B.C. rejoined. T.B.

Army Form C. 2118.

For # December
1917

WAR DIARY of Jodhpur C.Y.A

or

INTELLIGENCE SUMMARY.

(Erase heading not required.)

Instructions regarding War Diaries and Intelligence
Summaries are contained in F. S. Regs., Part II.
and the Staff Manual respectively. Title pages
will be prepared in manuscript.

Place	Date 1917	Hour	Summary of Events and Information	Remarks and references to Appendices
LE-MESNIL BRUNTEL	6th	—	Nothing to report — except that A.B.Corps Bearer No 7628 BADHAIN was admitted to the ambulance as a patient and transferred to the Lucknor C.C.S on 7th inst. N.B.	
	7th	—		
"	8th	—	No 7607 Bearer GHISA A.B.C. rejoined the unit from Base as a reinforcement. N.B.	
"	9th	—	Nothing to report. N.B.	
	10th	—		
	11th	—		
"	12th	—	Water cart sent in A.S.C. workshops 4th C.A.D. for repairs. N.B.	
"	13th	—	Motor ambulance No. 1866 broke its starting handle and was sent to workshops for repair. N.B.	
"	14th	—	Nothing to record. N.B.	
"	15th	—	Nothing to record. Sgt motor ambulance No 1866 returned from workshops duly repaired. N.B.	
	16th	—	This unit moved into its camp near DEVISE. N.B.	
DEVISE	17th	—	No 7628 Bearer Badhain rejoined.	
"	18th	—	Nothing to record. N.B.	
	19th	—		
"	20th	—	Water cart brought back from workshops, being repaired and No 7531 Naik GOPI, A.B.C. was sent to PARIS on 7 days leave. N.B.	
"	21st	—	Nothing to record. N.B.	
	22nd	—		
	23rd	—		
"	24th	—	Nothing to record except an/party of movement, officers on 2nd half, who found it though back to the unit. N.B.	
	25th	—		
"	26th	—	Nothing to record. The Workshop/party/Jodhpur cur. Bde. to camp West of VENDELLES. N.B.	

Army Form C. 2118.

For December WAR DIARY of Jodhpur C.H.

1917

INTELLIGENCE SUMMARY.

(Erase heading not required.)

Instructions regarding War Diaries and Intelligence Summaries are contained in F. S. Regs., Part II. and the Staff Manual respectively. Title pages will be prepared in manuscript.

Place	Date 1917	Hour	Summary of Events and Information	Remarks and references to Appendices
DEVSE	Dec. 26th	—	Naik Gopi A.B.C. returned from Paris leave. NB	
	27th	—	Nothing to record. NB	
	28th	—		
	29th	—	Wales cart returned to remts. NB	
	30th	—	Nothing to record. NB	
	31st	—	No 3441 Bearer Bhagat Ram 3⁵² L⁊ A.B.C. Transferred to No A. Battery R.H.A. 2ⁿᵈ	

W Southport Capt. I.M.S.
O.C. Jodhpur Cav. Fd Ambulance

4

Jodhpur Cas. F.A.

Jan. 1918

MEDICAL

ORIGINAL

for January 1916.

WAR DIARY of Jodhpur C.F.A.

INTELLIGENCE SUMMARY.

Army Form C. 2118.
Vol 37
235

Place	Date 1916 January	Hour	Summary of Events and Information	Remarks and references to Appendices
CAMP NEAR DEVISE	1st	—	Nothing to record. n.B.	
	2nd	—	No 4269 Br BHAGAT RAM A.B.C. evacuated and one of the ambulance cars (MT 1866) went in Workshops for dearhooving engine, repairs to spring and brakes etc. n.B.	
	3rd	—	Nothing to record. n.B.	
	4th	—	M2/032789 Pte Hughes, L.L. N.S.Corps M.T. evacuated sick. n.B.	
	5th	—	G.S. Limbers of this unit sent to Workshops A.S. Corps A.S.D. for urgently repairs n.B.	
	6th 7th 8th 9th	—	Nothing to record. n.B.	
	10th	—	Ambulance car (MT 1866) come back from Workshops supply col, with necessary repairs n.B.	
	11th	—	Nothing to record. n.B.	
	12th	—	G.S. Limber Wypon fetched back from Workshops dub repaired at 165 recent /039 water carried ZAHUR AHMED, Sweeper evacuated sick.	
	13th 14th 15th	—	Nothing to record. n.B.	
	16th 20th	—	Nothing to record. n.B.	
	21st	—	No 77360 Bearer BHOLA, A.B.C. 107 Coy A.B.C. joined as reinforcement. n.B.	
	22nd to 25th	—	Nothing to record. n.B.	

Army Form C. 2118.

WAR DIARY
INTELLIGENCE SUMMARY.

for January 1918.

(Erase heading not required.)

Instructions regarding War Diaries and Intelligence Summaries are contained in F. S. Regs., Part II. and the Staff Manual respectively. Title pages will be prepared in manuscript.

Place	Date Jan 1918	Hour	Summary of Events and Information	Remarks and references to Appendices
Camp near DEVIZES	26th	—	Ambulance car (MA 1858) c/o of A/Cpl Goodman A.S.C. M.T. detailed for duty - with 2n/o of 5th Cavalry Divisional School at DADURS. No 1924 Pack Store Harville SHAM SINGH 51st Sikhs, joined as reinforcement from Harville. N.B.	
	27th R	—	No 11142 N.O. Pannu Lal, detailed for duty with the Inchcock C.F.A. N.B.	Reg. letter from DAAG - G.H.Q. 3rd Echelon Indian Section No. 1/26+5/57 of 27 Dec. 1917 N.B.
	28th R	—	No 16869 Pack Store Harville TILOK SINGH R.H.A. Transferred to Base N.B.	
	29th R 30	—	Nothing to record. N.B.	
	31st	—	No T.4/254026 Driver General A. Grant A.S.C. H.T. T/341826 " " G. Park R.S.C. H.T. joined the unit as reinforcement from Base. N.B.	

W Bonford
Captain
O.C. Godhpur C.F.A.

A5834 Wt W4973/M687 750,000 8/16 D. D. & L. Ltd. Forms/C.2118/13.

Jodhpore Cav. F. A.

February, 1918.

Army Form C. 2118

WAR DIARY
or
INTELLIGENCE SUMMARY.
(Erase heading not required.)

January 1918

Instructions regarding War Diaries and Intelligence Summaries are contained in F. S. Regs., Part II. and the Staff Manual respectively. Title pages will be prepared in manuscript.

Place	Date 1918	Hour	Summary of Events and Information	Remarks and references to Appendices
ORESMAUX	8th to 12th R		Nothing to record. WJM	
"	13th		24 men of the Unit were inoculated against Typhoid fever. WJM	
"	14th		Two motor ambulances sent to D.C. 4th Cav. Div. Supply Column for exchange. Animals tested for glanders. WJM	
"	15th		Nothing to record. WJM	
"	16th		Ford new Ambulance cars (Sunbeam) W.D. Nos. AP 44125 and 44127, received in exchange. Nothing to record.	authority D.D.T.(s) 538/9
"	17th		Captain T.L. Bamford Ives, having proceeded on 14 days leave, struck over charge WJM	
"	18th		of ½ffm C.F.A. WJM ¾codnHawllam Captain Reine (S.R.)	
"	19th		Nothing to record. WJM	
"	20th		Nothing to record. WJM	
"	21st		11 men of the unit were inoculated against Typhoid fever. WJM	
"	22nd		Nothing to record. WJM	
"	23rd R		W.O. Panna Ål & Sowar Shimere Horse, rejoined. 24 men passed 2nd doze T.A.B. vaccine WJM	
"	24th		No T.4/85137 Driver Panirose, C. A/C. H.T. } No T/34/826 " Park, g. a.t.d. H.T. } Transferred to Ambala. C.F.A. WJM	
"	25th 26th 27th R		Nothing to record. WJM	

ORIGINAL

Army Form C.2118.

WAR DIARY of Jodhpur Cav. Fd. Ambulance, Medical – Vol. 38.

INTELLIGENCE SUMMARY

February 1918.

(Erase heading not required.)

Instructions regarding War Diaries and Intelligence Summaries are contained in F.S. Regs., Part II. and the Staff Manual respectively. Title pages will be prepared in manuscript.

Place	Date	Hour	Summary of Events and Information	Remarks and references to Appendices
Camp near DEVISE	1st	—	No. 2457 Ward Orderly RAM SINGH, 37th Lancers started from railhead being unfit for further active service, he is returning to India.	
"	2nd	—	Bearer No. 3288 LACHMAN) both 9th 3rd Coy A.B. Corps arrived " No. 3444 GANGA RAM) from the Base as reinforcements to this unit. NB.	
"	3rd	—	L/Cpnd Goodman ASC, MT, in charge of motor ambulance which was detached on duty elsewhere on 26th last month, returned to this unit. NB. One riding horse, with complete set of saddlery, strayed and is missing. NB.	
"	4th	—	Nothing to record. NB.	
"	5th	—		
"	6th	—	Eighteen dismounted men of this unit under Hovildar SHAM SINGH were sent to report to the Lucknow Cav. Fd. Ambulance, with whose dismounted men they will entrain tomorrow and be taken to new billeting area. The Ambulance marched at 7.45 am. via BRIE and the main AMIENS road to half-way billets at GUILLAUCOURT. NB.	
GUILLAUCOURT	7th	—	The Ambulance marched at 7.30 am. via VILLERS BRETTONEUX and southern outskirts of AMIENS to billets at ORESMAUX – arriving at 4.45 pm. The dismounted men had arrived earlier. NB.	

Army Form C. 2118.

War Diary of Godpur C.F.A.

for February 1918

INTELLIGENCE SUMMARY.
(Erase heading not required.)

Instructions regarding War Diaries and Intelligence Summaries are contained in F. S. Regs., Part II. and the Staff Manual respectively. Title pages will be prepared in manuscript.

Place	Date	Hour	Summary of Events and Information	Remarks and references to Appendices
ORESMAUX	28th Feby	—	One Cart store Vanillies and 15 bearers A.B.C. and 4 followers of stretchers, were sent to wilhens, being temporarily detached from the unit.	

W.M. Roder Hamilton
Captain Rowe (S.R.)
for O.C. godpur Cavalry Field Ambulance

www.ingramcontent.com/pod-product-compliance
Lightning Source LLC
Chambersburg PA
CBHW081243170426
43191CB00034B/2023